D0943823

BEAVERS

AND THEIR HOMES

Deborah Chase Gibson

The Rosen Publishing Group's
PowerKids Press™
New York

Published in 1999 by The Rosen Publishing Group, Inc.
29 East 21st Street, New York, NY 10010

First Edition

Book Design: Kim Sonsky

Photo Credits: Cover and title page © International Stock/Mark Newman; pp. 3, 22 © International Stock/Wayne Aldridge; pp. 4, 14 © International Stock/J. Robert Stottlemyer; pp. 5, 22 © Animals Animals/Alan G. Nelson; p. 6 © Animals Animals/Leonard Lee Rue III; p. 8 © FPG/Jeri Gleiter; p. 9 © International Stock/Ron Sanford; p. 10 © Animals Animals/Victoria McCormick; p. 12 © Animals Animals/Johnny Johnson; p. 13 © International Stock/Michael Lichter; p. 17 © Animals Animals/E. R. Degginger; p. 18 © Animals Animals/Harry Engels; p. 21 © Animals Animals/Marty Stouffer.

Gibson, Deborah Chase.
    Beavers and their homes / Deborah Chase Gibson.
        p. cm. — (Animal habitats.)
    Includes index.
    Summary: Presents an overview of the physical characteristics and habits of beavers and how and where they make their homes.
    ISBN 0-8239-5307-6
    1. Beavers—Juvenile literature. 2. Beavers—Habitat—Juvenile literature. [1. Beavers.] I. Title. II. Series: Gibson, Deobrah Chase. Animal habitats.
    QL737.R632.G53 1998
    599.37—dc21   98-5833
                                                                        CIP
                                                                         AC

Manufactured in the United States of America

CONTENTS

THE BEAVER

In the woods, you may see branches, mud, and rocks carefully mixed together across one end of a pond. You might wonder how it all got there. Well, you're probably looking at a **dam** (DAM) made by a beaver!

Beavers are the builders of nature. They can actually make ponds and lakes by building dams across streams, such as rivers and brooks. The ponds and lakes beavers make are their **habitats** (HA-bih-tats). They make their homes in the middle of the ponds and lakes. Beavers are found in Russia and North America.

Beavers move very slowly when walking on land. ▶

4

WHAT ARE BEAVERS LIKE?

Beavers belong to the same **species** (SPEE-sheez) of animals as mice. They are **rodents** (ROH-dents). They have thick brownish or black fur coats, and they can grow to be four feet long. Beavers are excellent swimmers. Their back feet are webbed just like a duck's. Beavers use their feet as paddles when they swim. Their broad, flat tails help beavers steer themselves through water.

Beavers are **nocturnal** (nok-TER-nul). That means that they are active at night and they rest during the day. Beavers don't have very good eyesight. But they can hear and smell very well. These things help them move around easily during the night.

◀ A beaver's powerful tail and webbed feet make it a great swimmer.

THE TEETH OF THE BEAVER

Beavers' most important building tools are their long front teeth: two on the top and two on the bottom. These teeth help beavers build homes in their habitats. Beavers cut down trees with these strong, sharp **incisors** (in-SY-zurz). They also use these teeth to munch off bark from trees.

Beavers' teeth never stop growing. But like all rodents, beavers chew often on hard **material** (muh-TEER-ee-ul). All of this tough chewing wears down beavers' teeth so they never grow too long.

Using their strong teeth, beavers can cut ▶ down small trees in minutes.

THE BEAVER POND

Beavers use their dams to make ponds so they can build a **lodge** (LAHJ), or home, in the middle of a pond. This lodge protects them from their **predators** (PREH-duh-terz), such as bears and coyotes. To make a pond, beavers first have to find a stream. Once they find a stream, beavers work together as a family. They all gather branches, mud, and rocks to build the dam across the stream.

A dam blocks the flow of water. When the water is blocked, it floods the land around it, making a pond. Beavers also build lodges in bodies of water that are already ponds. This raises the water level in the pond. A high water level keeps the pond safe from predators.

Beaver families work as a team when building a dam.

BUILDING THE DAM

To get tree branches for their dams, a group of beavers chew at the trunk of a tree until it falls over. Then they drag it to the spot where the dam is being built.

Beavers' front feet have five fingers. They use their feet to scoop mud from the bottom of the stream. They swim with the mud to the dam **site** (SYT). The beavers pack mud between the branches and rocks to make the dam strong. With a lot of branches, rocks, and mud, the dam becomes big and solid enough to stop the flow of water.

Beavers use their mouths and front paws to carry sticks and stones underwater to build their dams. ▶

THE BEAVER LODGE

A beaver lodge is an island of branches, mud, and rocks that is found in the middle or on the side of a pond. A lodge can be as high as six to ten feet above a pond's surface. Beavers build their lodges the same way they build their dams.

Beavers hollow out a living area inside their lodge. Beavers then pack the walls with mud so that the lodge stays warm, even in winter.

No matter how hard you look, you won't be able to find a lodge's entrance when you are standing on land. That's because the only way inside a beaver lodge is underwater. Beavers dive into the water and swim up through short tunnels that lead to the inside of the lodge. Their homes are built this way so that land predators can't get inside.

◄ There are usually several underwater passages that beavers must steer themselves through to get inside their lodge.

THE BEAVER FAMILY

When beavers **mate** (MAYT), they stay together their whole lives. Baby beavers live with their families for about two years. Older brothers and sisters help care for their younger **siblings** (SIB-lingz) by playing with them and watching over them. When baby beavers grow older, they go off to mate and to have families of their own.

In the fall, a beaver family stores food for the winter. They drag trees and shrubs into the water and store them in the mud near their lodge. In the winter, they swim out to get the food they need.

Beavers can stay underwater for as long as fifteen minutes. ▶

LIFE AROUND THE BEAVER POND

When beavers aren't busy building, they are busy eating. Bark, buds of trees, leaves, plants, and twigs are some of beavers' favorite foods. The part of the tree they don't eat, such as the trunk, is used for their lodges and dams. A beaver family also **forages** (FOR-ih-jez) in the pond for water lilies, moss, and ferns.

Beavers "talk" to each other a lot. They hiss when they are angry. When they eat together, they make noises at each other. If beavers sense danger, they slap the water with their tails. The loud whack of a beaver's tail warns other beavers in the area that danger is near.

During the cold months of winter, when there aren't any leaves or plants around, beavers eat only bark.

THE BEAVERS' ENVIRONMENT

No other animals can change their **environment** (en-VY-urn-ment) the way beavers can. As beavers flood the land where they're building a dam, the number of fish in the newly created pond grows. This means other animals, such as otters, will want to live there too.

The plant life around the pond also changes. Lilies and other water plants **thrive** (THRYV) in this new environment. Beavers cut down trees, and clearings are made. This lets more sunlight through for plants on the forest floor. Ponds can dry up if a beaver family moves away, but then that land often turns into a beautiful meadow.

Beavers create environments that attract more fish, new plants, and new animals, such as otters. ▶

BEAVERS AND HUMANS

People are the biggest danger to beavers and their habitats. Even though beavers' habitats are in and around ponds, beavers still cross paths with humans. Beaver ponds can flood roads, farms, and neighborhoods. This can cause problems for many people.

Scientists are working hard to find ways to protect beavers and their habitats. But people must learn to be patient and respect all animals and nature so we can live near each other in peace.

WEB SITES:

You can learn more about beavers on the Internet. Check out these Web sites:

http://www.ngpc.state.ne.us/wildlife/beaver.html

http://onlink4.onlink.net/home/norland/btale.htm

GLOSSARY

dam (DAM) Something that is used to block flowing water.

environment (en-VY-urn-ment) A place in which plants, animals, and humans live.

forage (FOR-ij) To hunt or search for food.

habitat (HA-bih-tat) The surroundings where an animal lives.

incisors (in-SY-zurz) An animal's four front teeth used for cutting.

lodge (LAHJ) A beaver's home.

mate (MAYT) A special joining of a male and female body. After mating, the female may have a baby grow inside her.

material (muh-TEER-ee-ul) What a thing is made from.

nocturnal (nok-TER-nul) To be active during the night.

predator (PREH-duh-ter) An animal that kills other animals for food.

rodent (ROH-dent) A kind of animal such as a mouse, a rat, or a squirrel.

sibling (SIB-ling) A brother or sister.

site (SYT) The place or position of something.

species (SPEE-sheez) A group of animals that are very much alike.

thrive (THRYV) To grow strong.

INDEX